Prehistoric Animals

ARMORED DINOSAURS

WINDMILL
BOOKS

New York

Published in 2016 by **Windmill Books**,
an Imprint of Rosen Publishing
29 East 21st Street, New York, NY 10010

Designed and illustrated *by* David West

Cataloging-in-Publication Data
West, David.
Armored dinosaurs / by David West.
p. cm. — (Prehistoric animals)
Includes index.
ISBN 978-1-5081-9014-1 (pbk.)
ISBN 978-1-5081-9015-8 (6-pack)
ISBN 978-1-5081-9016-5 (library binding)
1. Ornithischia — Juvenile literature. 2. Dinosaurs — Juvenile literature.
I. West, David, 1956-. II. Title.
QE862.O65 W47 2016
567.915—d23

Manufactured in the United States of America
CPSIA Compliance Information: Batch #BW16PK: For Further Information contact Rosen Publishing, New York, New York at 1-800-237-9932

Contents

Ampelosaurus

AMP-ell-uh-SAWR-us

This long-necked dinosaur is different from most of the dinosaurs in this book.

The one thing it does have in common with them is its spiky, armored skin. **Predators** such as a *Tyrannosaurus* would have found it difficult to chew its way through this armor.

Ampelosaurus means
"Vineyard Lizard."

Ampelosaurus grew up
to 49.2 feet (15 m) in
length and weighed
10 tons (9 metric tons).

Ampelosaurus was a
member of the giant,
long-necked dinosaurs
known as titanosaurs.

Ankylosaurus grew up to
23 feet (7 m) in length
and weighed 5.8 tons
(5.3 metric tons).

Ankylosaurus means
"Fused Lizard"
because of the
nodules "fused"
into its skin.

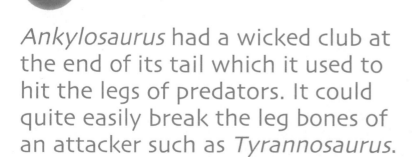

Ankylosaurus had a wicked club at
the end of its tail which it used to
hit the legs of predators. It could
quite easily break the leg bones of
an attacker such as *Tyrannosaurus*.

Ankylosaurus

ang-KILE-uh-SAWR-us

Ankylosaurus was protected from predators by thick, leathery skin from which grew bony, oval nodules called osteoderms.

With the discovery of more than 40 almost-complete skeletons, *Euoplocephalus* is the best-known ankylosaur among **paleontologists**.

Euoplocephalus grew up to 23 feet (7 m) in length and weighed 4 tons (3.6 metric tons).

Euoplocephalus

you-op-luh-SEF-uh-lus

Euoplocephalus was very similar to *Ankylosaurus*. It had a tail club and thick, leathery skin covered in bony nodules, some of which formed spikes. Even its eyelids were armored.

Euoplocephalus means "Well-armored Head."

Hungarosaurus grew up to 13.1 feet (4 m) in length and weighed 1,100 pounds (500 kg).

Hungarosaurus means "Hungarian Lizard."

Hungarosaurus

hun-ger-uh-SAWR-us

Hungarosaurus had excellent armor along the top of its body. It had two rows of sharp spikes growing from its neck to halfway down its tail. It had no tail club though.

Hungarosaurus had a strange shape. Its front legs were longer than its back legs.

Kaprosuchus

CAP-row-SOO-kuss

This ferocious, armored beast was not a dinosaur but a type of **crocodilian** that lived on land. It roamed the plains of Africa hunting plant-eating dinosaurs.

Kaprosuchus grew up to 20 feet (6.1 m) in length and weighed around 1,000–2,000 pounds (454–907 kg).

Kaprosuchus means "Boar Crocodile."

This scary beast had strange horns sticking out from behind its eyes and three sets of tusk-like teeth.

15

Pachycephalosaurus grew up to 15 feet (4.6 m) in length and weighed around 1,000 pounds (454 kg).

Pachycephalosaurus means "Thick-headed Lizard."

Pachycephalosaurus

pak-ee-SEF-uh-lo-SAWR-us

This dinosaur had a heavily armored head. It was not for protection. It used it to butt opponents during the mating season, like deer do today.

Paleontologists think their heads might also have been used in self-defense. Their hard skulls and spiky edges could have caused serious injuries to their attackers.

Polacanthus

poe-la-CAN-thuss

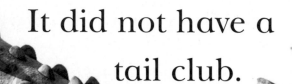

Polacanthus had a great armory of spikes and armor plates. It did not have a tail club.

If attacked by a predator, *Polacanthus* used its tail as a defensive weapon. As it whipped its tail sideways the spikes on the edges acted like hedge cutters!

Polacanthus means "Many Spikes."

Polacanthus grew up to 16.4 feet (5 m) in length and weighed 2 tons (1.8 metric tons).

Sauropelta

SAWR-oh-PEL-tah

This armored dinosaur had large spikes growing from its neck and shoulders. Its back was armored with thick, leathery skin studded with bony nodules.

If attacked by predators *Sauropelta* would lie down to protect its unarmored underside.

Sauropelta means "Lizard Shield."

 Sauropelta was 15 feet (4.6 m) in length and weighed 1–2 tons (0.9–1.8 metric tons).

21

Talarurus

tal-uh-ROOR-us

Although similar to an *Ankylosaurus*, this armored plant eater was slightly smaller. It had bony nodules embedded in thick, leathery skin, and a wicked clubbed tail.

 Its armored tail, held rigid by stiff tendons, had a club of fused bones at its end. Strong muscles at the base of the tail allowed it to be swung with great force at an attacker such as *Tarbosaurus*.

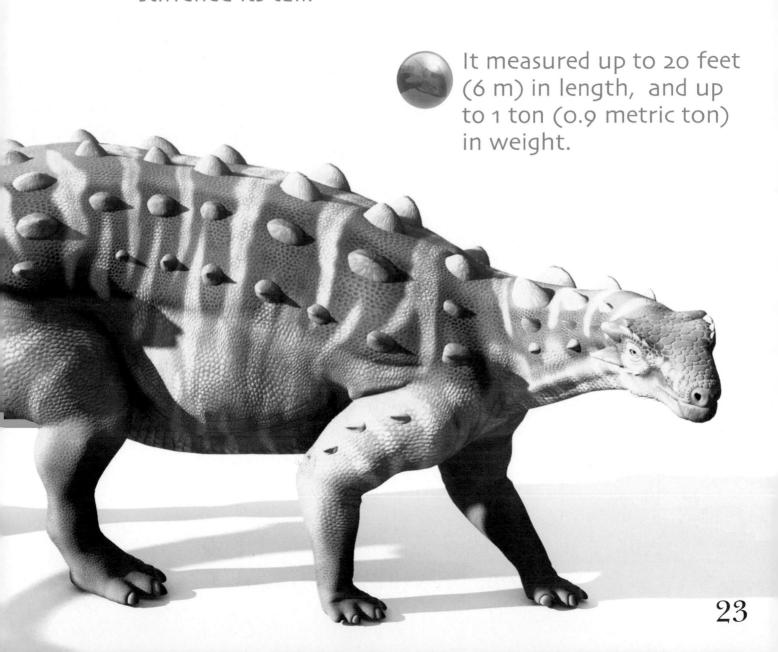

 Talarurus means "Wicker Tail" from the **wicker**-like tendons that stiffened its tail.

It measured up to 20 feet (6 m) in length, and up to 1 ton (0.9 metric ton) in weight.

23

Glossary

crocodilian
Of a group of animals that includes modern and ancient crocodiles.

predators
Animals that hunt and kill other animals for food.

paleontologists
Scientists who study early forms of life, chiefly by examining fossils.

wicker
Pliable twigs woven to make items such as furniture and baskets.

Timeline

Dinosaurs lived during the Mesozoic Era, which is divided into three main periods.

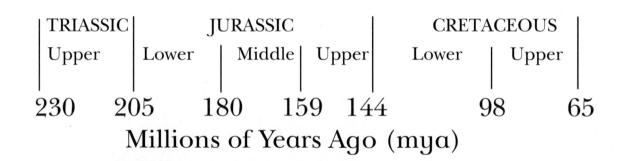

TRIASSIC	JURASSIC			CRETACEOUS	
Upper	Lower	Middle	Upper	Lower	Upper
230	205	180	159	144	98	65

Millions of Years Ago (mya)